Wonderful Nature,
Wonderful You

To my nieces, Zoë and Marriah Vinson. To children everywhere,
I support you in knowing the magic that you are. — *Karin Ireland*

To my dear friend, Dr. Jerry Mallet and the staff, docents,
and friends of the wonderful Mazza Collection for their dedication,
commitment and passion towards enriching the lives of all people
through the arts and children's literature. — *Christopher Canyon*

Published by DAWN Publications
14618 Tyler Foote Road
Nevada City, CA 95959
916 478-7540

Printed on recycled paper using soy based ink

Printed in Hong Kong

10 9 8 7 6 5 4 3 2 1
First Edition

Designed by LeeAnn Brook Design
Type style is Tiepolo

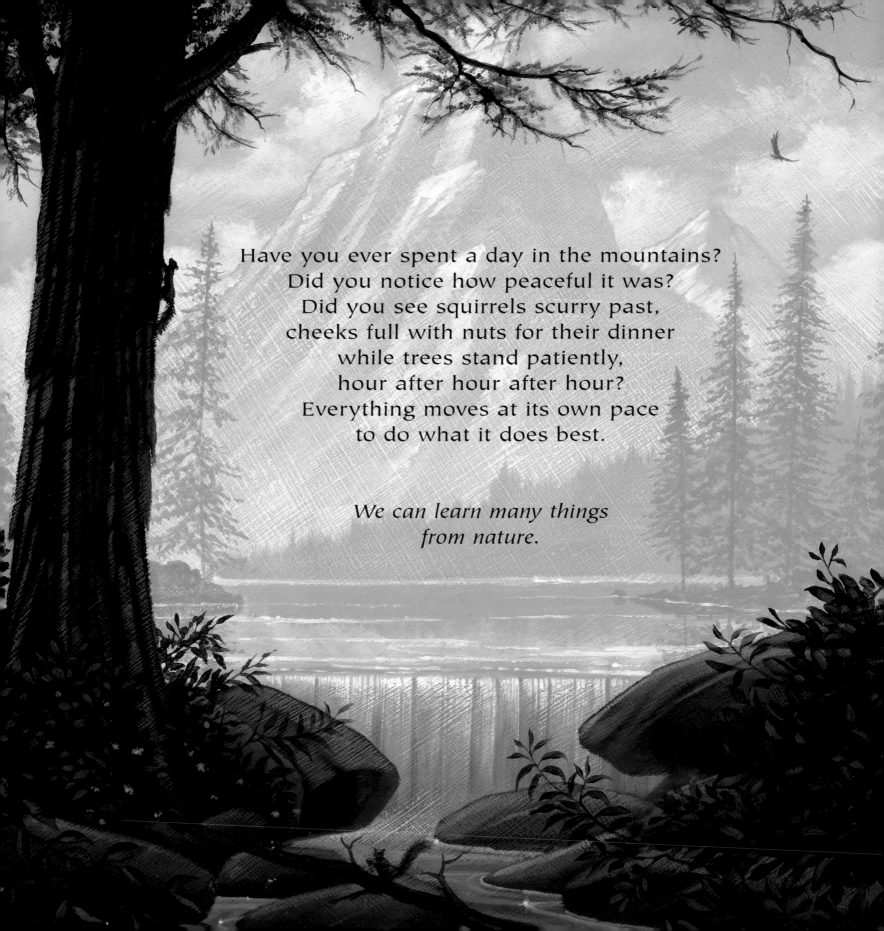

Have you ever spent a day in the mountains?
Did you notice how peaceful it was?
Did you see squirrels scurry past,
cheeks full with nuts for their dinner
while trees stand patiently,
hour after hour after hour?
Everything moves at its own pace
to do what it does best.

*We can learn many things
from nature.*

The sun doesn't struggle to move faster
or shine more brightly, but it never stops
moving or shining, either.
Stars don't try to change their patterns
to be more beautiful.

Coyotes howl, rabbits hop,
and opossums carry their babies
in a pouch.

It's okay to be different.
Everything in nature is perfect,
just the way it is.

You are perfect, too,
just the way you are.

Opossums are marsupials, which means they carry their babies around in a pouch. 'Possums often have as many as 14 babies at one time. When they're born, the kits are really only 13-day-old embryos the size of a bee. They are hairless and blind. Still, they manage to pull themselves through their mother's fur to her pouch where they can stay warm, nurse, and enjoy a free ride.

After about two months they climb out and ride on her back for a few weeks while they learn to find food. Actually, they don't have much to learn. 'Possums will eat just about anything.

Elephants are the only animal with a trunk.
The trunk is a combination of nose and upper lip. The trunk helps them
reach leaves at the top of trees that other animals aren't tall enough to reach.

The African elephant is the biggest land animal alive today. One of the largest ever
measured was more than 13 feet tall and weighed 22,000 pounds! Adults eat more
than 400 to 500 pounds of grass or leaves every day. If you think they must be eating
all the time, you're right!

As many as 14 females, or cows, and their youngsters live together and the oldest
cow is the leader. Elephants are very affectionate. After they have been separated,
family members greet each other with caresses and happy rumbles.

Fish don't try to walk
just because they see that birds can.

Elephants don't try to fly
and warthogs don't try to climb trees.

Tigers have stripes, leopards have spots,
and lions don't have either.
None wishes they were different.

Each is satisfied with the special gifts it has.

*You have special gifts, too,
and they are wonderful!
What do you think they are?*

Baby caterpillars don't come from grown-up caterpillars; they hatch from eggs the size of a pin head that are laid by butterflies.

Most caterpillars have eight pairs of legs. They don't have a nose or ears. They have a dozen eyes, placed in half circles on either side of their tiny head. Still, they are nearly blind. But since they can eat the leaves they stand on, they don't need to see much.

A few weeks after hatching, the caterpillar goes into an inactive state. Its soft skin hardens. After a couple of weeks it has changed and when it pushes through the shell, a beautiful butterfly flies away.

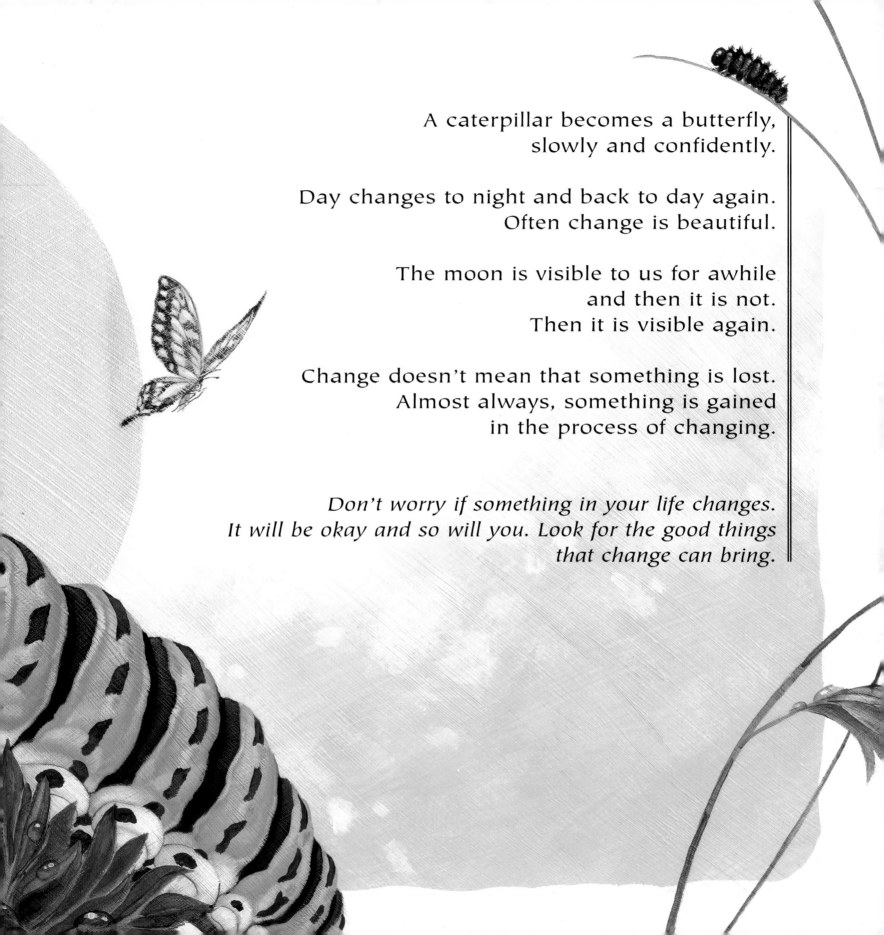

A caterpillar becomes a butterfly,
slowly and confidently.

Day changes to night and back to day again.
Often change is beautiful.

The moon is visible to us for awhile
and then it is not.
Then it is visible again.

Change doesn't mean that something is lost.
Almost always, something is gained
in the process of changing.

Don't worry if something in your life changes.
It will be okay and so will you. Look for the good things
that change can bring.

Sea otters like to have fun, juggling rocks or shells, playing tag and doing somersaults in the water. But they have work to do, too. Otters have two layers of fur that they must constantly groom. This grooming keeps their fur fluffy, which helps them stay warm in the cold water.

Sea otters are one of the few animals that know how to use tools. They often carry a flat rock with them and when they find a tasty abalone or clam, they roll onto their back, put the rock on their belly and bang the shell against the rock until it breaks open. Then they eat the soft meat inside.

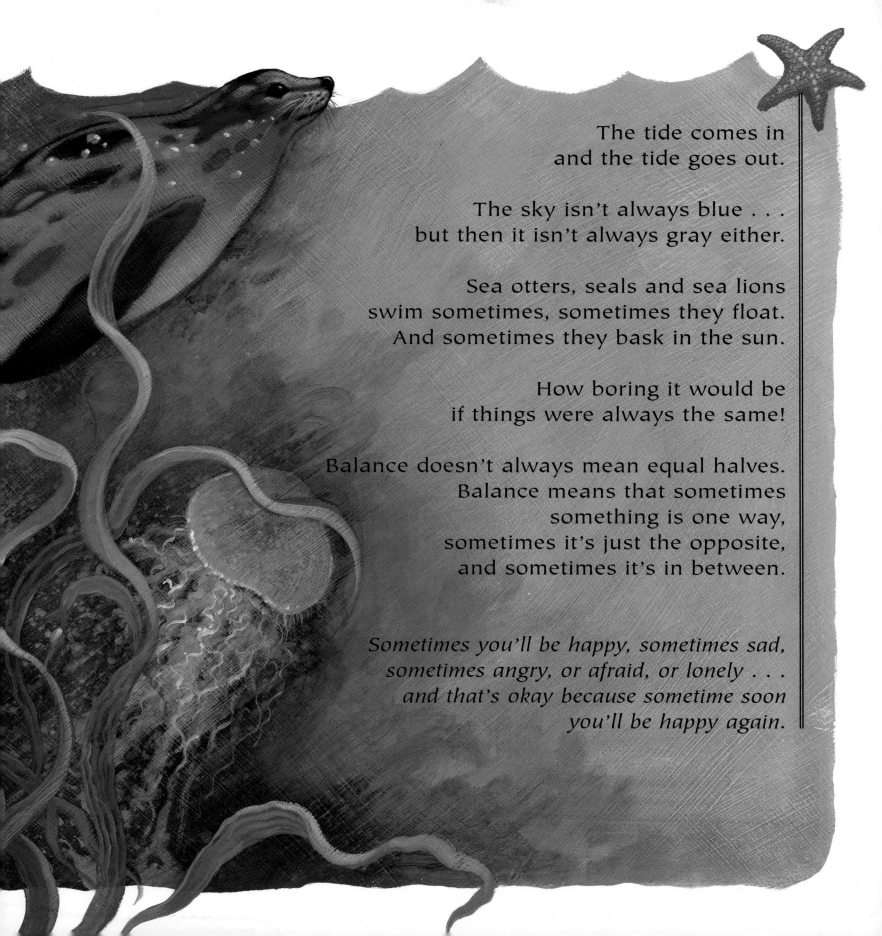

The tide comes in
and the tide goes out.

The sky isn't always blue . . .
but then it isn't always gray either.

Sea otters, seals and sea lions
swim sometimes, sometimes they float.
And sometimes they bask in the sun.

How boring it would be
if things were always the same!

Balance doesn't always mean equal halves.
Balance means that sometimes
something is one way,
sometimes it's just the opposite,
and sometimes it's in between.

*Sometimes you'll be happy, sometimes sad,
sometimes angry, or afraid, or lonely . . .
and that's okay because sometime soon
you'll be happy again.*

These small members of
the whale family are playful
and friendly. Often they swim
near boats, putting on a show
for people onboard. If a dolphin
is ill or injured the others will stay
with it for days, helping it to the surface every few minutes so it can breathe.
Dolphins have been known to push humans
who are drowning up to the surface, too.

Dolphins look like fish but they are really
mammals. They can stay under water for about 15
minutes, but then must come to the surface to breathe.

Dolphins have excellent hearing. They are very intelligent
and communicate in a series of chirps, clicks, whistles and
moans that scientists wish they could understand.

Whooping cranes dance
just for the fun of it,
leaping and bowing to their partner,
tossing bits of straw in the air
and catching it again.

Dolphins play
by leaping and diving
and then leaping and diving
again and again,
and using their bodies like surfboards
to ride the waves.

When you are playing, play with all your heart.
Don't worry about things that happened yesterday.
Don't worry about things that might happen tomorrow.
Think about what you're playing and enjoy yourself.

A snake doesn't rush to shed its skin too soon.
It couldn't, even if it tried!

A tadpole doesn't hurry to become a frog.
But it doesn't try to stay a tadpole forever, either.

Always do the best you can.
Don't rush to get something done
if it needs to be done slowly.
And don't take all day if what you're doing
needs to be done in a hurry.

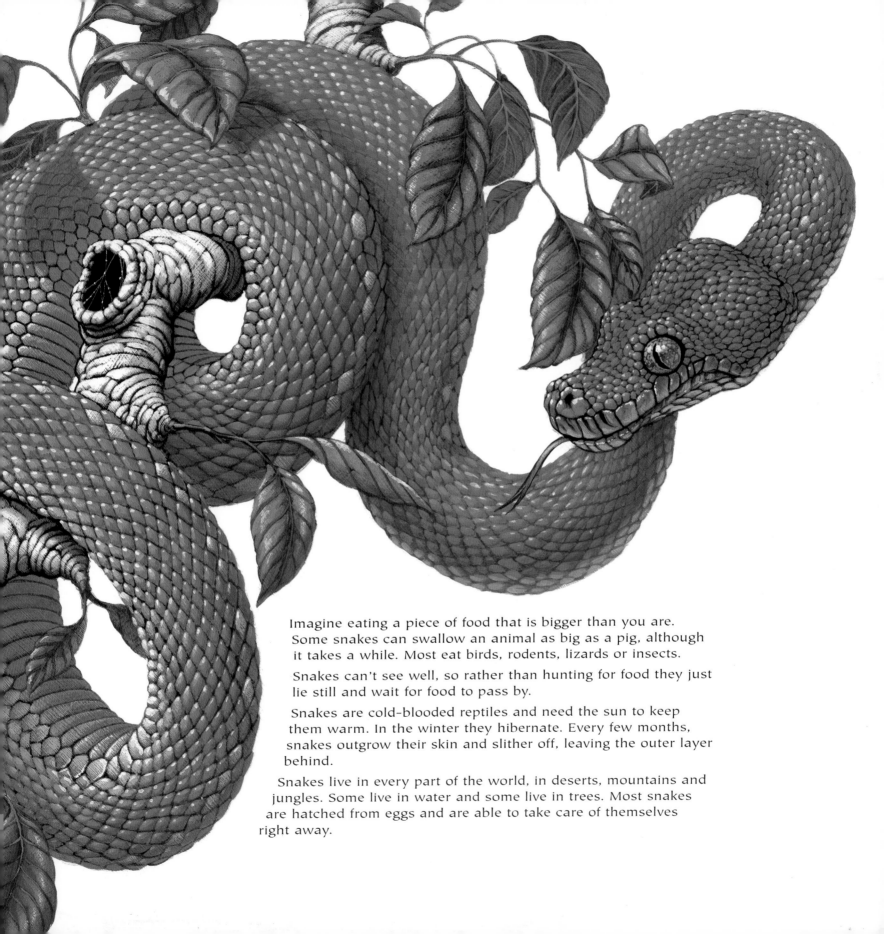

Imagine eating a piece of food that is bigger than you are.
Some snakes can swallow an animal as big as a pig, although
it takes a while. Most eat birds, rodents, lizards or insects.

Snakes can't see well, so rather than hunting for food they just
lie still and wait for food to pass by.

Snakes are cold-blooded reptiles and need the sun to keep
them warm. In the winter they hibernate. Every few months,
snakes outgrow their skin and slither off, leaving the outer layer
behind.

Snakes live in every part of the world, in deserts, mountains and
jungles. Some live in water and some live in trees. Most snakes
are hatched from eggs and are able to take care of themselves
right away.

Nothing says that all birds have to act alike.
Some eat fish and some eat fruit,
others eat seeds or worms or snails.

Some birds fly and some birds don't,
and some birds even swim.

They don't question their instincts,
each just does what feels right.

You don't have to be like somebody else
if it doesn't feel right to you.
You know how to be yourself
better than anybody else does.

Most birds fly, and their bones are honeycombed with air spaces to make them lighter.

Some birds know they aren't meant to fly and they don't try. One is the ostrich. An African ostrich is the largest bird in the world, at eight feet tall and more than 250 pounds. Its bones are solid so it can run to escape danger and protect itself with its powerful kick.

Another bird that doesn't fly is the penguin. Penguins look awkward walking on land but their bodies are perfect for swimming — smooth and sleek, with wings like paddles that help them glide through the water.

Gorillas are gentle, unless threatened.
They are peaceful and playful.
They don't get angry or fight,
except to protect themselves.

Giraffes never bother the grass-eating animals
that wander through their herds.
They will protect their babies
with a powerful kick to anyone who would harm them,
but they are really peaceful animals
who would rather run from danger than fight.

You, too, can decide what's important
to make a fuss about and what isn't.
Probably you'll discover that most of the time
it's more pleasant to be peaceful.

Gorillas can act very fierce, screaming and beating their hands against their chest. But unless something is trying to hurt them, they are peaceful and almost shy.

A baby gorilla behaves a lot like a human baby. It is almost completely helpless when born and the mother carries it all the time. As a youngster, it plays most of the day, wrestling, climbing trees and sliding down branches with its friends.

Gorillas are very smart. One gorilla was taught American Sign Language, which was created for people who cannot hear. She knows nearly 500 words. When asked if she is an animal or a person, Koko makes the hand signs for, "Fine animal gorilla."

The average lion doesn't know anything about fairness. It knows that sometimes it catches dinner and more often than not, dinner gets away. A lion wouldn't blame another lion if it were unable to catch a wildebeest. It wouldn't blame itself either.

If the grass isn't tall enough where zebras are grazing, they move until they find grass more to their liking.

If the lake or river dries up, hippopotamuses travel to another lake or river and make their home there.

If you try something and it doesn't turn out the way you wanted, that's okay. Don't blame someone else, and don't be angry at yourself. Just try again.

Lions are good hunters and can run very fast, but most of the animals they feed on can run faster. Most prey will fight back when lions attack. Hunting is hard work and dangerous. People who study these large cats say that 70 to 80 percent of the time the lions' dinner escapes.

Lions only hunt when they're hungry. They spend the rest of their time lying in the shade. Some climb trees and rest in the branches. They're not lazy, but food is hard to get and they need to save their energy to catch the next meal.

The flowing river makes holes in the homes and dams beavers build and so they must stay busy patching and rebuilding.

Ants can carry pieces of food that weigh more than they do.
If they find an obstacle in their path they don't give up. They find a way to get past it and do what they set out to do.

Don't you give up, either. If you do something and it doesn't work the first few times, try doing it a little differently.

Beavers like to live where the water is deep and slow, and if there isn't a pond nearby, they make one by blocking a river.

Some beavers dig homes in the river banks and others build their lodges in the middle of a pond. These dome-shaped homes may rise four feet above the water and look like a jumble of debris. But they are really very comfortable homes with a living area above water that's carpeted with dry leaves. Tunnels all open below water so family members can come and go without being seen by predators.

A green sea turtle returns to the beach
were it was hatched to lay its own eggs.
The beach may be several hundred miles
away. But when it's time to migrate,
the turtle simply begins its trip.

When it's time for a baby parrot
to fly, it spreads its wings
and flies.

Nature expects to succeed
in doing what it's there to do.

*You can do anything you set
your heart and mind to do.
You really can.*

Green sea turtles swim several hundred miles to reach the beach where they were hatched so they can mate and lay eggs. It may have been two or three years since they were there and the journey can take up to eight weeks. How do they find their way? Maybe they use the stars to guide them.

A female may bury as many as a hundred eggs on the beach. After about two weeks, babies will poke out of their shells. It may take them days to dig their way up through the sand and then they must find the ocean. Most that hatch will die. It isn't easy being a baby sea turtle.

Nature is an expert at recycling. When animals die in the wilderness, they become food for other meat-eating animals. Even small bugs can be food for other bugs. Anything that isn't eaten becomes fertilizer to help feed the plants.

When a plant dies it eventually falls to the ground. It may take years, but the sun and rain will soften the branches, and they will break apart and become nourishment for the soil.

In nature, dying is part of life.
Flowers, trees and animals
live for awhile
and then they die
to make room for other flowers,
trees and animals to live.

When something dies, though,
it never really goes away.
It changes form
from what it was
to something that still exists
but is different.

Have you ever had a pet that died?
It's normal to feel sad.
But the pet will always be there in your memory
and in your heart.

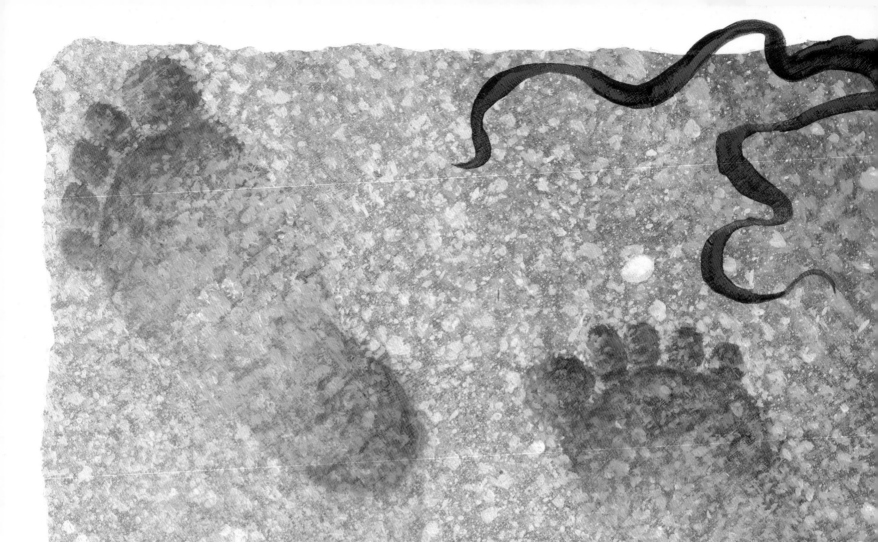

Nature does not hope that it will be okay.
Nature doesn't need to hope,
because it seems to know that it is perfect,
whole and complete just the way it is
and just the way it isn't.

And so are you!

It knows it already has everything it needs to succeed.

And so do you.

About this book

Young children are full of enthusiasm and optimism, limitless curiosity, and a sense of being competent to take on all challenges. This book supports them in remembering how terrific they are and offers messages that are empowering.

At the same time, it entertains them with fun facts about nature and encourages them to look and think about what they see, probably in ways they haven't done before.

Some children will prefer to listen to the story passively, simply absorbing the information. Others will enjoy thinking and talking about how each section applies to their own lives so the book becomes interactive. Many will enjoy doing both at different times.

Through the examples of nature, **Wonderful Nature, Wonderful You** encourages children to trust themselves, to believe in themselves and to have fun.

P.S. The messages are great for grownups, too.

About the Author and Illustrator

Karin Ireland grew up in Southern California where her first memories of nature were of digging huge holes in the dirt at the back of the yard, climbing trees and eating berries fresh from the vine.

This is Karin's tenth book and one that is especially meaningful because of the empowering messages it offers. These are the same messages she used to move from a life of struggle and frustration to one of peace and (most of the time) contentment.

On Valentine's Day, 1995, she left a job and a condo in California to live her dream in Hawaii.

Christopher Canyon is the illustrator of four books for children. When he isn't in his studio, Christopher enjoys traveling and providing educational and entertaining programs for schools, libraries, and conferences. Christopher received his formal art education at the Columbus College of Art & Design in Columbus, Ohio. His work has been selected for many exhibits and publications including the Society of Illustrators, the Mazza Collection at the University of Findlay, Ohio and Natural History magazine. His first book with DAWN Publications, **The Tree in the Ancient Forest**, has won a Ben Franklin Award for best children's picture book of the year.

Christopher lives with his wife and cat in central Ohio.

Acknowledgments

I'd like to thank Glenn Hovemann, a very special editor, for seeing the possibilities in the very first draft, Pauline Handin for loving it long ago, Dr. George Losey, Professor of Zoology at the University of Hawaii, Manoa, for giving the initial project his nod of approval, Tom Higashino, Assistant Director of the Honolulu Zoo, for his comments on the final draft, and, as always, Tricia Ireland, daughter extraordinaire and my favorite first reader, for her wise insights and constant support — *Karin Ireland*

I would like to give special thanks to my wife Jeanette, my family, and all of my great friends at DAWN Publications for their love, enthusiasm, patience and appreciation of my work.
— *Christopher Canyon*

DAWN Publications is dedicated to helping people experience a sense of unity and harmony with all life. Each of our products encourages a deeper sensitivity and appreciation for the natural world. For a copy of our free catalog listing all of our products, please call 800-545-7475. Please look at our web site at www.dawnpub.com for more information.